Living with Death

Activities to Help Children Cope with Difficult Situations

For Primary Grades

by
Mary Jane Cera, M.Ed.

illustrated by Charles Ortenblad

Cover by Paul Manktelow

Copyright © Good Apple, 1991

ISBN No. 0-86653-588-8

Printing No. 987654321

Good Apple
1204 Buchanan St., Box 299
Carthage, IL 62321-0299

The purchase of this book entitles the buyer to duplicate the student activity pages for classroom use only. Any other use requires written permission from Good Apple.

All rights reserved. Printed in the United States of America.

Simon & Schuster Supplementary Education Group

Author's Note

This book was written out of the growing need for children to know true facts about death as well as honest answers to their questions about dying, death and possible life after death. This book has three basic parts.

The first section is a children's story entitled "My Dad Is Dead—but Not Forgotten." This story is intended to act as a vehicle for discussion regarding the death of a close family member.

The second section encourages the child to write her/his own story about the life and death of a loved one. The activities in part two are identified with hearts (♥).

The third section provides further activities to assist the child to clarify his/her beliefs and values related to life, death and possible life after death. The activities in part three are identified with dots (●).

It is my sincerest hope that the activities in this book will assist adults to help children to participate appropriately in the death experiences of life and the life experiences of death.

Mary Jane Cera

In Memory Of

Danny Kinerk (May 17, 1962-September 5, 1980)
Leslie Bressert (January 27, 1963-August 25, 1981)
John Piel (March 6, 1969-September 19, 1981)
Michele de Tiege (February 4, 1970-April 25, 1982)

Because of you, we emerge with a greater understanding of death and a greater commitment to life.

This book is written to the memory of Sam Cera: husband, father, grandfather and brother to many people who love him deeply and remember him dearly.

In Appreciation

I would like to thank Judy Bisignano for her assistance and encouragement in writing this book and allowing me to use essential concepts from the book she authored of this same title that is written for older children and adults.

I would also like to thank Lee and Debbie Bergman, Alice Paul and Jenna Orzel for portraying with compassion and sensitivity the family in the story "My Dad Is Dead—but Not Forgotten."

Assisting Children to Live with Death

Adults must play a significant role in assisting children to live with death. The most important thing adults can do is to help children understand and accept their feelings throughout the entire death experience. The following information is intended to assist you in this effort.

1. Children need to learn how to mourn, that is, to go through the process of giving up some of the feelings they have invested in an animal or person and go on with other and new relationships. They need to remember, to be touched by the feelings generated by their memories. They need to struggle with real or imagined guilt over what they could have done. They need to deal with their anger over the loss.

2. Children need to mourn over the small losses, such as plants and animals, in order to deal better with larger, closer losses of people.

3. Children need to be informed about a death. If they aren't told but see that adults are upset, they may invent their own explanations and even blame themselves.

4. Children need to understand the finality of death. Because abstract thinking is difficult for them, they may misunderstand if adults say that a person or animal "went away" or "went to sleep." If you believe in an afterlife and want to tell your child about it, it is important to emphasize he/she won't see the person or animal again on Earth.

5. Children need to say good-bye to the deceased by participating in viewings and/or funerals, if only for a few minutes. No child is too young to participate in these activities.

6. Children need opportunities to work out their feelings and deal with their perceptions of death by talking, dramatic playing, reading books or expressing themselves through the arts.

7. Children need reassurance that the adults in their lives will take care of themselves and probably won't die until after the children are grown. However, children need to know that everybody will die someday.

8. Children need to know that other children die, but only if they are very sick or if there is a bad accident. It is equally important that they understand that almost all children grow and live to be very old.

9. Children need to be allowed to show their feelings: to cry, become angry or even laugh. The best approach is to empathize with their feelings. For example, you might say, "You're sad. You miss Grandma. Tell me about it."

10. Children need to feel confident that their questions will be answered honestly and not avoided. They need to know that adults will give them answers they can understand. Adults should take their cues from the children and answer only what they ask.

Developmental Stages

Children go through a series of stages in their understanding of death. Most children between the ages of 2 and 4 see death as reversible, temporary, and impersonal. Watching television cartoon characters rise up miraculously after having been blown apart tends to reinforce this notion.

Between the ages of 5 and 9, most children begin to realize that death is final and that all living things die. They still do not see death as personal They hold the notion that they can escape death through their own ingenuity and efforts.

From age 9 or 10 through adolescence, children begin to comprehend fully that death is irreversible, that all living things die, and that they too will die someday. Many teenagers become intrigued with seeking the meaning of life and developing philosophical views of life and death.

Time Intervals for Mourning

In helping older children deal with death, it may be important to be aware of critical time intervals related to mourning. Mourning is the process whereby children work through the death of a loved one, thus regaining a sense of balance in their lives. Mourning is a functional necessity, not a weakness. It is a form of healing. Adults need to create the opportunities for children to be able to share their needs with us so we can assist them in living with death.

During the first twenty-four to forty-eight hours, the impact of the reality of death occurs. For the next five to six days, one may experience a mild depressive reaction to this reality. The next six to eight weeks is the most difficult adjustment period. The impact of the death of a loved one hits with acute symptoms of anxiety and depression such as loss of sleep, overeating or lack of appetite, weeping, fatigue, acute mood swings, and decreased ability to concentrate and remember.

At about three months, the mourning person may experience irritability and complaining, physical and verbal acting out of anger and frustration, crying, and physical complaints such as headaches, backaches, diarrhea, etc. At about six months, depression is a common occurrence with repeated depression at about twelve months. From twelve to twenty-four months, the mourning person usually arrives at an acceptance of the death or a resolution of the grief. Mild recurrent depression is often associated with the anniversary of the death of a loved one. Years after the death of this person, mild depression often occurs on special dates such as birthdays and holidays. These feelings and critical time intervals related to the mourning process may vary considerably for different people.

My Dad Is Dead but Not Forgotten

Even though it has been two years, it is still hard to believe my dad is dead. It is sometimes hard to believe that he is not ever coming home again. I still miss my dad, and I will always remember him.

Everyone said I looked just like Dad. We had the same big brown eyes. We had the same black hair. We even sat the same way when we read the comics in the Sunday paper.

Dad and I took care of the garden in our backyard. We planted tomatoes, beans, onions and radishes. We planted geraniums, too. We fixed the soil just right. We pulled all the weeds. We watered our garden every day.

During the summer, Dad and Mom and I had the best salads you ever tasted.

Dad and I played in our backyard. He showed me how to hit a baseball. I learned to hit the ball way over his head.

He showed me how to play marbles like he did when he was a young boy.

Dad knew how to make things out of wood. He made a box for me to keep all of my special things.

He carved a dog for me, just like the one we saw in our favorite movie.

Dad was a great cook. He made all kinds of great tasting things, but his chocolate brownies were my favorite. He made them just right.

We both liked to listen to music. We both liked to go camping in the woods. We both liked to drink root beer floats.

But my favorite time with Dad was listening to him read a story right before I went to sleep.

One day when I came home from school, Grandma was there. She told me that Dad got sick at work and that Mom had taken him to the hospital.

Mom came home late that night and said that Dad was very sick. She said that his heart was not working well and that he might not get better.

I said "No!" I did not believe Mom. I knew Dad would get better and come home.

But Dad did not get better. The next day Mom came home from the hospital. She was crying. She said that Dad had died. Grandma cried, too.

I went out in the yard. I didn't cry, but I felt bad and scared. Who would be there to help me learn new things and to take me places?

Grandma tried to explain that my dad was with my grandpa. I didn't want Dad with Grandpa. I wanted him with me.

In a little while, many people came to our house. Some of them cried. They all talked about Dad and the things he used to do and say. I just sat and listened.

In a few days, there was a funeral service for Dad. More people talked about him. Someone said prayers. Someone played Dad's favorite song on the organ.

After the funeral service, we all went to the cemetery. I put a geranium from the garden on Dad's grave.

In a few days, I went back to school. I didn't feel like doing much. I didn't want to play baseball or marbles with my friends. I didn't even want to drink root beer floats.

One day, after a long time, I came home from school. Mom was looking at some old photographs. She asked me if I would like to look at the pictures with her.

We found lots of pictures of Dad . . . when he was a boy . . . when he and Mom married . . . when I was born. We found lots of pictures of Dad and me.

We looked at pictures for a long time. We laughed at the one of Dad trying to fix the broken garden hose. Mom told me I could keep many of my favorite pictures of Dad.

All at once I felt like crying. I held Mom and Mom held me. We cried together for a long time. Later, Mom said that crying makes you feel better when you are sad.

A few days later, Mom and I went to the garden, and we fixed it together.

That night Mom read a story to me before I went to sleep. Now she often reads to me at night.

Grandma and I make chocolate brownies. They taste almost as good as the brownies Dad used to make. Grandma said that's because she taught Dad how to make brownies. She said she would teach me, too.

Mom never did learn to play baseball, but this year I joined a team with my friends.

I still play marbles and listen to music and drink root beer floats. Once in awhile I even go camping in the woods. It's not the same, but it's good.

I keep my pictures of Dad in the special box he made for me. Sometimes I put the carved dog in my pocket just to carry it with me.

I still miss Dad. I miss him at Christmas when we decorate our tree. I miss him on his birthday. I miss him in the summer when we grow our garden. I guess I'll always miss him.

A lot of time has passed. I can remember and talk about Dad without it hurting like it did when he died. I remember the things he taught me and the things he gave me. I remember the love we shared together. These things make me feel good.

I look back on the good times. I look ahead to the good times. I am happy. Dad would want it this way.

Reviewing the Story

1. What are some things the girl in this story enjoyed doing with her dad?

   _____
   _____
   _____
   _____
   _____

2. What are some things you enjoy doing with your mom or dad?

   _____
   _____
   _____
   _____
   _____

3. Why do you think the girl felt scared when her dad died?

   _____
   _____
   _____

4. How do you think the girl felt when her grandma told her that her dad was with her grandpa?

   _____
   _____
   _____

5. When did the girl finally feel able to cry about her dad?

   _____
   _____
   _____

6. What did the girl do to help herself accept her dad's death?

_____
_____
_____
_____

7. What did other people do to help the girl accept her dad's death?

_____
_____
_____
_____

8. Name some people that you can go to when you have a problem.

_____
_____
_____
_____

9. Tell about one of the happy times you have had with your mom or dad.

_____
_____
_____
_____
_____
_____

Remembering a Special Person

You may want to ask an adult to help you make a book about a special person in your life who has died. Your book might include some of the following ideas:

♥ Draw this person. Include as many details as possible about how this person looked.

♥ In words, describe the physical appearance of this person.

♥ Tell about the things this person liked to do. Draw a picture of this person doing one of these favorite things.

♥ Tell about some things that this special person has taught you. Draw a picture of yourself doing one of these activities that you learned.

♥ Name a favorite place where this special person could often be found. Draw a picture of this person in this special place. Tell what this person did in this favorite place.

♥ In pictures and in words, tell about a special day, moment or time that you shared with this person.

♥ Describe the memories and feelings you had when this special person died.

♥ Ask a parent or relative if you can have some photographs of this special person in your life. Paste the pictures in your book. Describe each photo.

♥ Tell about the special talents and gifts this person brought to your life. Tell about the special gifts that you bring to the lives of the people whom you love and who love you.

♥ Share your thoughts and feelings by writing a letter to this special person.

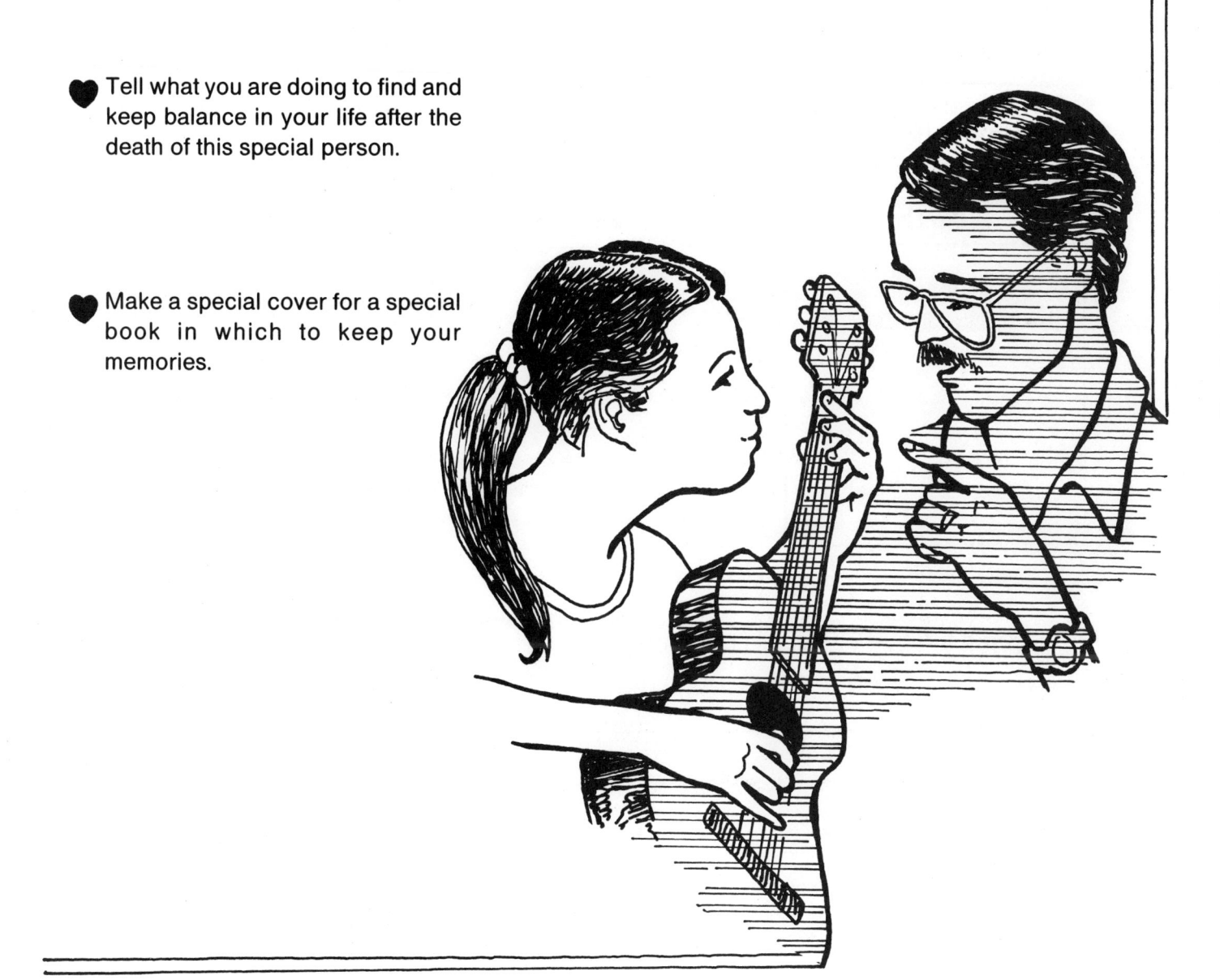

♥ Tell what you are doing to find and keep balance in your life after the death of this special person.

♥ Make a special cover for a special book in which to keep your memories.

It is hoped that the following activities will help you learn more about life, death and possible life after death.

Life and Death in Nature

Nature teaches us about life and death. Nature teaches us that every living thing is born, grows and dies. Nature also teaches us that every living thing has a purpose. For example, an acorn sprouts and grows into an oak tree. The oak tree gives shade and beauty while it is living. It also gives seeds for new living trees to sprout and grow. One day the tree dies. It decomposes and returns its nutrients to the soil to help other trees grow.

- Give an example of something in nature that is living. Draw a picture of its birth, growth and death.

Birth　　　　　　　**Growth**　　　　　　　**Death**

- Tell about the purpose of this living thing.

_____
_____
_____
_____
_____
_____

Purpose for Living

Just as in nature, every person has a purpose for living. Your purpose for living is what is special about you that you give to the people you love and who love you. Tell about your special gifts and talents that you bring to those around you.

_____
_____
_____
_____
_____
_____
_____
_____
_____
_____
_____
_____
_____
_____
_____
_____
_____
_____
_____
_____
_____
_____
_____
_____
_____

Picturing Life

- Find pictures and words in magazines that show life. Display them in the space below.

Picturing Death

- Find pictures and words in magazines that show death. Display them in the space below.

Death of a Pet

The death of a pet is often a very hard time for those who loved their pets.

Tell about the life of your pet.

_____
_____
_____
_____
_____

Tell about the death of your pet.

_____
_____
_____
_____
_____

Tell how you felt at the death of your pet.

_____
_____
_____
_____
_____
_____
_____

Tell what you did when you felt very sad about the death of your pet.

_____
_____
_____
_____
_____

Tell what you remember most about your special pet.

_____
_____
_____
_____
_____

Paste a photo of your pet in the space below.

Share with a friend the life and death of your pet.

Living Better—Not Longer

Imagine being told that you have six months to a year to live. How would you feel? Shocked? Mad? Sad? Would you be jealous of those people who still have a long time to live? Would you try to do a lot of things or just quit trying?

Tell how you would feel and what you would do if you had six months or a year to live.

_____
_____
_____
_____
_____
_____
_____
_____
_____
_____
_____
_____
_____
_____
_____
_____
_____
_____
_____
_____
_____
_____
_____
_____

Living Today

If you had only five days to live, how would you spend those days? With whom would you spend those days?

_____
_____
_____
_____
_____
_____
_____
_____
_____
_____
_____
_____
_____
_____
_____
_____
_____
_____
_____
_____
_____
_____

Why wait? You may want to make your five dream days happen now.

Visiting a Mortuary

Visit a mortuary. A mortuary is also called a funeral home.

- Ask the mortician to explain what he/she does.

- Visit the different rooms of the mortuary. Listen to the explanation of each room.

- Ask the mortician to explain cremation, when the body is burned and the ashes are usually buried.

- Ask the mortician to tell you about funeral preparations and expenses.

- Below, tell about your trip to the mortuary.

Visiting a Cemetery

a. Go to a cemetery. Ask the proprietor of the cemetery to explain what he/she does. What are the jobs of other people who work at the cemetery?

b. Improve the appearance of the cemetery or a particular gravesite in some way.

c. While visiting the cemetery, look at tombstones and read the different epitaphs. An epitaph is the writing on a tombstone in memory of the person buried there. In the space below, write an epitaph you saw.

___

d. Write an imaginary story about the life of this person.

___

Designing Your Tombstone

Design your own tombstone. Write your epitaph on your tombstone.

Obituaries

An obituary tells about a person's death. It usually tells something about the life of the person.

Read or listen to some obituaries in the newspaper. Cut out some obituaries of interest to you and paste them below.

Life After Death

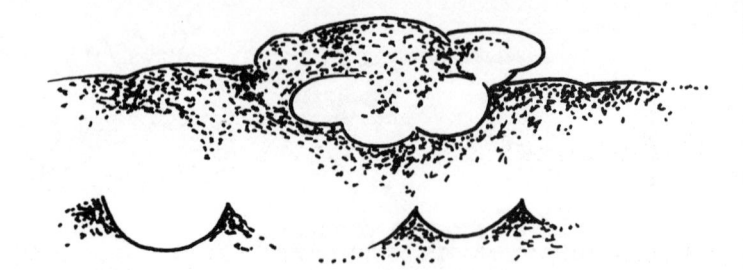

Many people believe that within each person there is a "spirit." They believe that this "spirit" or "soul" leaves the body when a person dies and goes to another place.

- If you believe that a person's spirit lives on after death, draw a picture of what you think this place looks like.

- Describe, in words, what you think life after death is like. (If you do not believe in life after death, explain why you have this belief.)

_____
_____
_____
_____
_____
_____
_____
_____
_____
_____
_____
_____

- Ask your mom or dad to explain what life after death must be like. (If he/she does not believe in a life after death, ask him/her to explain why he/she has this belief.)

_____
_____
_____
_____
_____
_____
_____
_____
_____
_____
_____
_____

Ten Guidelines for Living with Death

1. **ACCEPT YOUR SORROW.** Do not try to be brave. Take time to cry. Crying is not a sign of weakness. It is a natural expression of sorrow.

2. **TALK ABOUT IT.** Find a family member or friend to talk to. Your friends may act embarrassed at first. You can help them and you by talking about the death of your loved one. Find someone who has experienced a similar sorrow. Talk often.

3. **KEEP BUSY.** Do the usual things that keep you busy.

4. **EAT WELL.** Your body needs good nourishment during this time of sadness.

5. **EXERCISE REGULARLY.** Exercise will help you sleep better and keep your mind healthy. Do your normal exercise or start a new physical activity.

6. **ACCEPT YOUR UNDERSTANDING OF THE DEATH.** You have probably asked "why" over and over and have gotten no satisfying answer to your question that you feel sure about. You probably understand a little why someone died. This answer is okay for now. Some questions have no answers.

7. **GIVE OF YOURSELF.** Find a way to help others. Helping someone else will probably help you feel better.

8. **KEEP A JOURNAL.** Write or draw your own thoughts in a journal. This may help you get your feelings out.

9. **FIND STRENGTH INSIDE YOURSELF.** Spend some time alone bringing peaceful thoughts to your mind. If you pray, praying to God for peace may help.

10. **GET HELP.** If you are not able to stop feeling sad or angry, find an adult to talk to who can help you or get help for you.

Bibliography

Books on death and dying can provide children with answers to questions that they may not know how to ask. Books can also provide the impetus for children to reveal their own thoughts and feelings as well as provide the framework for adult-child discussions about dying and death.

Before introducing a book about death to a child, it is very important that the teacher or parent first read the book. Familiarity with the book will assist the adult in answering questions a child may have. It will also allow the adult to determine if a book's content is consistent with one's own belief and approach to death—if such consistency is a necessary adult value.

Books for Children Ages 3 to 7

Aliki. *The Two of Them.* New York: Greenwillow Books, 1979.
    Called "A Poem of a Picture Book." The author captures true, lasting love of a grandparent and child in the markings of time—of life and death. A poem of meaning for adults and children to share together.

Buscaglia, Leo. *Freddie the Leaf.* Holt, Rinehart and Winston, 1982.
    A delightful book whereby Freddie compares the seasons of the year with the life-death cycle. Not until Freddie falls from the tree does he realize the fullness of life he has had.

Carrick, Carol. *The Accident.* New York: Clarion Books, 1976.
    The accident wasn't anyone's fault, but at first Christopher blamed the driver who hit Bodger. Later he blamed himself. But no matter whom he blamed, nothing would bring Bodger back.

Cohn, Janice. *I Had a Friend Named Peter.* Wm. Morris & Co., Inc., 1987.
    A sensitive story about the accidental death of a little girl's best friend, and the parents and teacher who help her to understand what has happened. Includes a parent/teacher guide to answering children's questions about dying, funerals and the burial process.

Coutant, Helen. *First Snow.* Alfred A. Knopf Publishers, 1974.
    A six-year-old Vietnamese girl, Lein, learns the meaning of death during her first snow. With the help of her grandmother, Lein begins to understand death as a natural part of life.

DePaola, Tomie. *Nana Upstairs, and Nana Downstairs.* New York: G.P. Putnam's Sons, 1973.
    Told in simple language and very readable to young preschoolers, this is a pictured example of caring for and looking after the very old. When death comes, a little boy learns its meaning.

Graeber, Charlotte. *Mustard.* New York: Macmillan Publishing Company, 1982.
    When the vet diagnoses a heart ailment in Mustard the cat, eight-year-old Alex, with the help of his family, must come to terms with Mustard's increasing infirmities and eventual death.

Kubler-Ross, Elisabeth. *A Letter to a Child with Cancer.* Escondido, California: Shanti Nilaya, 1979.
   The author writes to a nine-year-old boy with cancer and answers his three questions: What is life? What is death? Why do young children have to die?

_____. *Remember the Secret.* Millbrae, California: Celestial Arts, 1982.
   Suzy and Peter are best friends with each other and their two unseen companions. Suzy is faced with the reality of Peter's death. When he joins their supposedly imaginary companions, there is sadness, but also wisdom and victory.

Miles, Misaka. *Annie and the Old One.* Little, Brown and Company, 1971.
   A beautiful story of a little Navajo Indian girl, Annie, who is given a weaving stick by her grandmother. Annie's grandmother is old and predicts that she will die and "return to mother earth" when the rug has been woven. To postpone her grandmother's death, Annie undoes the weaving already done. Her grandmother explains that one cannot change the order of nature and Annie begins to weave again.

Nobisson, Josephine. *Grandpa Loved.* San Diego: The Green Tiger Press, Inc., 1989.
   The boy tells how Grandpa loved the beach and showed the boy how to love it, too. The same with the wind, the woods, the animals, the city, the people and especially the family. When death comes, the boy concludes that Grandpa can go anywhere and see anything—the wind, the animals, the people and the family he loved and who loved him. Colorful, realistic illustrations.

Prestine, Joan Singleton. *Someone Special Died.* Los Angeles: Price, Stern, Sloan Publishers, Inc., 1987.
   Young Rick tells what it feels like to have his best friend die. He is lonely, sad and angry. As he makes a scrapbook of memories, he slowly comes to accept his friend's death. The engaging illustrations and simple text make the story easy for young children to understand.

Sanford, Doris. *It Must Hurt a Lot.* Portland, Oregon: Multnomah Press, 1986.
   A story about the sudden death of Joshua's dog, Muffin, and the lessons Joshua learns about life and death. The lessons are called his "special secrets" and are spelled out in useful ways that can help young children deal with death.

Thurman, Chuck. *A Time for Remembering.* New York: Simon & Schuster, Inc., 1989.
   A boy sits by the fireplace, holding the faded yellow flower that his grandfather gave him before his death. The voices in the next room make the boy feel warm in a different way from the fire. The boy fondly remembers his grandfather, places the flower in the fire and joins his family and friends.

Varley, Susan. *Badger's Parting Gifts.* New York: Lothrop, Lee & Shepard, 1984.
   Badger was a friend, and almost everyone who knew him had warm and loving memories of when he was living with them. At first, those who loved Badger were overwhelmed by his death. In time, though, whenever Badger's name was mentioned, someone would recall something about him that made everyone smile. Badger was part of their lives once more.

Viorst, Judith. *The Tenth Good Thing About Barney.* New York: Atheneum, 1972.
   When Barney the cat dies, his young owner tries to think of ten good things to say at the funeral, but he can only think of nine. As he helps his father in the garden, he realizes that Barney will now help the flowers grow—the tenth good thing. A warm and honest book.

Books for Children Ages 8 to 14

Blume, Judy. *Tiger Eyes.* New York: Dell Publishing Company, Inc., 1981.
    Davey can't believe that her father has been shot to death in a holdup at his 7-Eleven store. With her mother near collapse and her brother, Jason, too young to understand, Davey and the family move to New Mexico to stay with relatives and try to recover from the shock. Davey discovers a private place in the depths of the Los Alamos Canyon where she begins to put the pieces of her life back together.

Forrai, Marie, and Anders. *Rebecca, A Look at Death.* Minneapolis: Lerner Publications Company, 1978.
    The book is a description of the concepts of death through words and photographs. It relates the importance of grief and the customs of mourning.

Hyde, Margaret D., and Lawrence E. Hyde. *Meeting Death.* New York: Walker & Co., 1989.
    A straightforward presentation of death-related facts and concepts. Provides information to promote the acceptance of the concept of death, discussing such aspects as the terminally ill, suicide, grief and mourning, and the treatment of death in various cultures. Includes a chapter on helping children deal with a parent's death.

Jury, Mark, and Dan Jury. *Gramp.* New York: Viking, 1976.
    A photo history of the life of Frank Tugend and of his death at age 81. Follows him through the good old days, then into his three years of deteriorating mental and physical health, and then his death. It is a realistic look at Frank's failing health and death, as photographed and narrated by those who loved him.

Lee, Virginia. *The Magic Moth.* Seaburg Press, 1972.
    This is a story about Mark-O, age 6, and his family, who comes to understand the illness and eventual death of his ten-year-old sister, Maryanne. As Maryanne gets weaker and weaker from heart disease, the father explains to the older children that she is going to die. They work through their feelings as a family and are present when Maryanne dies at home.

Le Shan, Eda. *Learning to Say Good-Bye.* New York: Macmillan Publishing Company, 1976.
    The author discusses the questions, fears and fantasies children may have about the parent who has died. The different stages of mourning are discussed. You learn not just about death and grieving, but about life itself.

Mann, Peggy. *There Are Two Kinds of Terrible.* New York: Doubleday & Company, Inc., 1977.
    A very readable story for adolescents. It is a moving story of how a young boy faces the death of his beloved mother and must now learn to relate to his withdrawn and sorrowful father.

Mellonie, Bryan, and Robert Ingpen. *Lifetimes: A Beautiful Way to Explain Death to Children.* New York: Bantam Books, 1983.
    A moving book for children of all ages. It lets us explain life and death in a sensitive, caring way. It tells about beginnings, endings and living in between. With large, wonderful illustrations, it tells about plants, animals and people. It tells that dying is as much a part of living as being born. It explains how all living things have their own *Lifetimes.*

Norris, Louanne. *An Oak Tree Dies and a Journey Begins.* New York: Crown Publishers, Inc., 1979.

>A scientific account of the ways in which a tree, even after it dies, continues to be an important part of our environment.

Smith, Doris B. *A Taste of Blackberries.* Thomas Y. Crowell, 1973.

>Jamie fooled around a lot, so when he rolled on the ground after a bee sting, his friend thought he was joking. But Jamie died and the friend felt guilty and responsible. The age-old question of "why" is answered by a neighbor who says, "One of the hardest things we have to learn is that some questions do not have answers."

Vogel, Ilse-Margaret. *My Twin Sister Erika.* New York: Harper & Row, 1976.

>A story for elementary-aged children but poignant to all in the sorrowful loss and slow adjustment to the death of a twin sister. Appropriate to any brother and sister loss.

White, E. B. *Charlotte's Web.* New York: Harper & Row, 1952.

>This is an animal fantasy about friendship between Charlotte, a spider, Templeton, a rat, and Wilbur, a pig. When Charlotte dies at the fairgrounds, her friends manage to take her eggs to the farm where they can safely hatch.

Books for Teenagers and Adults

Bluebond-Langner, Myra. *The Private Worlds of Dying Children.* Princeton, New Jersey: Princeton University Press, 1978.

>The author shares her experiences with leukemic children. She explains how children know they are going to die and how they adapt to the death-denying society in which they live out their courageous journey to death.

Bombeck, Erma. *I Want to Grow Hair, I Want to Grow Up, I Want to Go to Boise.* New York: Harper & Row, 1989.

>A heartwarming account of kids surviving cancer. America's favorite family writer brings us the stories of children who have every hope of beating the odds and living to drive their parents crazy. The reader will smile at their wisdom, be dazzled by their insights and share the joys of their triumphs. It is not a medical book, nor is it a sad book. It sparkles with innocence and glistens with hope.

Conley, Herbert N. *Living and Dying Gracefully.* New York: Paulist Press, 1979.

>Reflections of the author's own impending death and how these meditations helped him to live a richer, fuller life.

Fulton, Robert. *Death and Dying: Challenge and Change.* Reading, Massachusetts: Addison-Wesley, 1978.

>Deals with intricate issues of death and dying as found in articles from newspapers and books. Provides a comprehensive overview of death as encountered in modern-day society.

Grollman, Earl. *Concerning Death: A Practical Guide for the Living.* Boston: Beacon Press, 1974.

>Deals with the facts and emotions of death. A practical guide in planning funeral services and making wills.

———. *Explaining Death to Children.* Boston: Beacon Press, 1967.

>Provides information and practical guides for parents to communicate with their children and help them understand death.

_____. *Talking About Death: A Dialogue Between Parent and Child.* Boston: Beacon Press, 1970.
> A sensative approach toward helping parents deal with a difficult subject. Perceptive and tender as a lyric poem, the author gently guides the reader in coming to terms with death—one of life's processes.

_____. *What Helped Me When My Loved One Died.* Boston: Beacon Press, 1981.
> Offers loving support to those who having lost a loved one feel totally alone. It defines the pain of loss and offers constructive ways of coping with the separation of a loved one.

Hamilton, Michael, and Helen Reid. *A Hospice Handbook: A New Way to Care for the Dying.* Grand Rapids: Wm. Eerdman, 1980.
> A succinct and a valuable guide to a greater understanding and appreciation of the hospice movement.

James, John W., and Frank Cherry. *The Grief Recovery Handbook.* New York: Harper & Row, 1988.
> A novel approach to the resolution of grief as practiced by the authors in their roles as grief counselors. In partnership with one or more other grievers, one reviews past losses and the ways in which those losses were resolved. Honesty and free expression of emotions, no matter how long they have been smothered, are the keys.

Kastenbaum, Robert. *Psychology of Death.* New York: Springer, 1972.
> An excellent resource for every library. Gives a comprehensive review of various aspects of death.

Kavanaugh, Robert. *Facing Death.* New York: Penguin, 1974.
> A compelling book that forces the reader to examine his attitudes about death. Discusses such issues as euthanasia, suicide and the value and purpose of funerals.

Kubler-Ross, Elisabeth. *Living with Death and Dying.* New York: Macmillan Publishing Company, 1981.
> An insightful book that causes the reader to take a serious look at the Gospel message regarding the sick and the dead. The author's work spans a decade of caring for the terminally ill, including the total needs unique to the dying.

_____. *Questions and Answers on Death and Dying.* New York: Macmillan Publishing Company, 1974.
> A selection of the author's most frequently asked questions and candid answers about dying. It's a sequel to *On Death and Dying* and covers such topics as the dying person, suicide, funerals and problems encountered by the family of the dying person.

Schweidman, Edwin. *Death: Current Perspectives.* Palo Alto, California: Mayfield Press, 1976.
> A compilation of changing trends in thanatology. Provides a broad summary of contemporary insights about death and dying.

Smith, Kathleen. *The Stress of Sorrow.* Dallas, Texas: Southwest Book Services, 1978.
> Treats death as a process of lift. Graphically describes all phases of sorrow including, in a sensitive way, the unique grief and sorrow associated with suicide, murder, abortion.

Service Organizations for Death Education

Candlelighters Childhood Cancer Foundation
1312 18th Street N.W., Suite 200
Washington, D.C. 20036
(202) 659-5136
An international organization for parents of children with cancer.

The Center for Attitudinal Healing
19 Main Street
Tiburon, CA 94920
(415) 435-5022
A family center that also supports group meetings of children who have to face life and death situations because of their illnesses.

Children's Hospice International
1101 King Street, Suite 131
Alexandria, VA 22314
(703) 684-0330
An international organization that encourages hospice care of terminally ill children as an alternative to the traditional institutional system.

Compassionate Friends
P.O. Box 3696
Oak Brook, IL 60522
(708) 990-0010
National organization offering emotional and educational support to families with children who have died.

The Elisabeth Kubler-Ross Center
Headwater, VA 24442
(703) 396-3441
A nonprofit, nonsectarian organization dedicated to the enhancement of life and growth through the practice of unconditional love.

Make a Wish Foundation
1624 E. Meadowbrook
Phoenix, AZ 85016
(602) 248-9474 (WISH)
Fulfills favorite wish of any child under eighteen who has a life-threatening illness.

Parents of Murdered Children
100 E. 8th Street, B-41
Cincinnati, OH 45237
(513) 721-5683
An ongoing support group for families who have lost a child, parent or spouse by murder.

Pen Pals for Terminally Ill Teenagers
Teenagers can write:
"Pen Pal," KCAL TV
5515 Melrose Avenue
Los Angeles, CA 90038